D1708885

THE RISE AND FALL OF EMPIRES™

THE RISE AND FALL OF THE MING DYNASTY

DANIEL R. FAUST

ROSEN
PUBLISHING

Published in 2017 by The Rosen Publishing Group, Inc.
29 East 21st Street, New York, NY 10010

Library of Congress Cataloging-in-Publication Data

Names: Faust, Daniel R., author.
Title: The rise and fall of the Ming Dynasty / Daniel R. Faust.
Description: First edition. | New York : Rosen Publishing, 2016. | Series:
  The rise and fall of empires | Includes bibliographical references and
  index. | Audience: Grade 7 to 12.
Identifiers: LCCN 2015048429| ISBN 9781499463484 (library bound) |
ISBN
  9781499463460 (pbk.) | ISBN 9781499463477 (6-pack)
Subjects: LCSH: China—History—Ming dynasty, 1368-1644.
Classification: LCC DS753 .F38 2016 | DDC 951/.026—dc23
LC record available at http://lccn.loc.gov/2015048429

Manufactured in China

CONTENTS

INTRODUCTION

Modern China is the fourth largest country in the world by area, and the largest by population, with a vast and diverse landscape that includes deserts, mountains, steppes, and subtropical forests. The people of China are equally diverse, coming from ethnic groups like the Han, the Khitan, the Mongols, and the Manchu. The history of China reflects this diversity. Since around the seventeenth century BCE, China has been ruled by successive dynasties, or lines of rulers from the same family, culture, or ethnic group.

China was ruled by a number of dynasties of varying lengths. Beginning in the early 1200s, China was invaded by the Mongols. By 1279, the Mongol ruler Kublai Khan established the Yuan dynasty. One hundred years later, a peasant uprising would lead to the overthrow of the Yuan and the establishment of the Ming dynasty. The Ming would lead China into another golden age.

Under the Ming, China would see rapid population growth and urbanization, the growth of private industry, improvements in agriculture, and the expansion of foreign trade into the Indian Ocean and East Africa. During this time, a series of older walls and fortresses were connected to form the Great Wall of China. The Ming also moved China's capital from Nanjing to the newly constructed Forbidden City in Beijing. The Ming dynasty had a strong and complex central

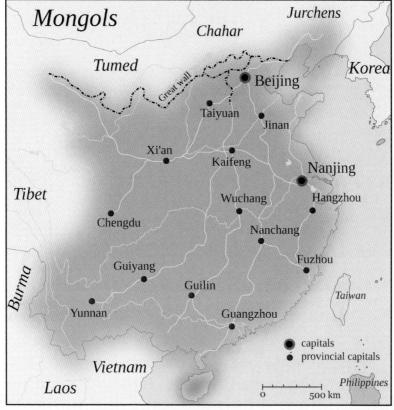

Known as the Empire of the Great Ming, China under the Ming dynasty stretched from the Great Wall in the north to what is present-day Vietnam in the south.

government, a standing army of over one million soldiers, and the largest navy in the known world.

Despite its many accomplishments, the Ming dynasty would not remain in power forever. In 1618, the Ming dynasty fell to the Qing, or Manchu, dynasty from Manchuria in what is now northeastern China. The Ming dynasty would be the last imperial dynasty ruled by ethnic Han Chinese. Even after its decline, the legacy of the Ming dynasty endures to this day. The period's art, architecture, philosophy, and literature continue to have a cultural impact on China and the rest of the world.

CHAPTER 1

THE NORTHERN DYNASTY, THE SOUTHERN DYNASTY, AND THE MONGOL INVASIONS

For much of its history, the Chinese state faced the threat of invasion from the Mongols. The Mongols were nomadic warriors from the steppes, a flat, grassy region that stretched from Asia into central Europe. For several thousand years, the Mongols rode across central Asia, conquering nearby towns and cities. The Mongols were nomadic pastoralists, moving their herds of horses, goats, sheep, camels, and cattle from one grazing spot to another. For centuries, the Mongols battled various groups, including the ancient Greeks, the Romans, the Persians, the Arabs, and the Chinese.

In the thirteenth century, under the leadership of Genghis Khan and his descendants, the Mongols spread out to the south and west, quickly building an empire that would eventually stretch from eastern Europe to Korea. Although the Mongol Empire would soon split into four mini empires, it was the largest land empire to be controlled by a single family of rulers. Moreover, it was the largest to be controlled by nomadic peoples.

MONGOL CONQUEST: KUBLAI KHAN AND THE YUAN DYNASTY

Beginning in 1207, the Mongols, under their leader Genghis Khan, began a series of invasions into northern China. At that time, China was not one unified country, but a series of smaller empires. Genghis Khan led an initial invasion of Western Xia in northwestern China in 1207. The Mongols withdrew in 1208, only to return one year later. The Mongols' larger campaign into Western Xia in 1209 was more successful. The Mongols conquered several cities along the Yellow River, eventually laying siege to the capital, Yinchuan. In 1210, the Western Xia submitted to the Mongol invaders, becoming vassals of the growing Mongol empire.

After subduing the Western Xia, the Mongols

The Mongols were fierce warriors who were feared throughout most of central Asia. This 16th-century Persian illustration shows a Mongol siege of a Chinese fortress.

turned their attention to the Jin empire. Between 1211 and 1212, the Mongols led a series of raids into Jin territory in northern China and Manchuria, the homeland of the Jurchen people, the ethnic group that ruled the Jin empire. Beginning in 1214, Genghis Khan led his Mongol troops in an invasion of the Jin empire that would last several years. The Mongols found unexpected allies in their war against the Jin: rebels from the Han Chinese and Khitan people, two other ethnic groups in northern China. By 1234, the Mongols had destroyed both the Jin and the Western Xia, effectively conquering northern China.

Although the Mongols ruled northern China, the Song dynasty still held southern China, presenting a continuing

threat to Mongol rule. After three decades of war, the Mongols eventually defeated the Song, reuniting China under a single ruler for the first time in centuries. In 1272, Genghis Khan's grandson, Kublai, founded the Yuan dynasty and declared himself emperor of China, which included what

Kublai Khan (1215–94) was the fifth Great Khan of the Mongol Empire. He became the first Mongol emperor of China when he founded the Yuan dynasty in 1272.

would become modern Korea and Tibet. This would be the first time that China was ruled by a foreign dynasty.

LIFE UNDER MONGOL RULE

As a nomadic people, the Mongols were not used to ruling a vast empire of farms and cities. Mongol rulers would often adapt to the local customs of the cultures they conquered, including their system of government. Mongol rule in China was no different. Establishing a new dynasty illustrated Kublai Khan's desire to have Mongol rule viewed as a legitimate successor to the dynasties of the past. Kublai Khan, known by the imperial name Yuan Shizu, had a deep respect for, and interest in, Chinese culture. The Yuan dynasty attempted to retain as much of the culture and government of southern China and the Song dynasty, while also solidifying Mongol authority. This combination of Chinese and Mongol influences created a sort of hybrid society that, at least superficially, resembled what had come before.

As Kublai Khan's chief Chinese advisor, a former Buddhist monk named Liu Bingzhong is said to have told the new emperor "although the empire had been conquered on horseback, it could not be administered on horseback." The Yuan dynasty retained much of the traditional form of Chinese government. The khan retained the three branches of government—the civil, the military, and the censorial—as well as a prime minister and the Six

Ministries. The prime minister advised the emperor on political policy, drafted laws, and oversaw the Six Ministries: the Personnel, Revenue, Rites, War, Justice, and Works. Kublai also adopted many of the ceremonial and religious rites that were part of traditional court life during China's imperial age. One aspect of traditional Chinese rule that Kublai Khan did not restore was the examination system that had been used to select officials for civil positions. The examinations were based on knowledge of the Chinese philosophy of Confucianism, and Kublai Khan felt that would limit his choice of officials.

Despite the outward resemblance to traditional imperial government, the need to appease a greedy Mongol aristocracy led to the creation of a system of government that resembled the feudalism that existed in Europe at the time. The population was divided into four groups. The Mongols sat at the top of the social hierarchy, with the "diverse peoples" (or *semu*) of central and western Asia, including Tibetans, Muslims, and Persians, right below them. The third group consisted of the Han people of northern China, which included the Khitan, Jurchen, and the people of Korea. Those from the former Song territories of southern China were the lowest group. The Mongols and the *semu* enjoyed legal and economic privileges, as well as preferred access to government jobs. Furthermore, political control of China was divided among local and provincial governments that were often ruled by Mongol aristocrats.

ZHU YUANZHANG AND THE PEASANT UPRISING

Despite Kublai Khan's reverence for traditional Chinese culture, his successors refused to follow suit, creating a feudal China that was divided along ethnic lines. Later Yuan emperors rewarded relatives and retainers with privileges and advancements, while essentially ignoring the population of ethnic Chinese, leading to an unhappy and rebellious peasant class. Unhappiness with Mongol rule, combined with a series of natural disasters and epidemics during the 1340s would eventually lead to the downfall of the Yuan dynasty.

The earliest indication that the Yuan dynasty was in decline was the rise of countless bands of armed men in the Yangtze and Huai River valleys. One of these bands, the Red Turbans, combined aspects of Taoist, Buddhist, and Manichean beliefs. Their dissatisfaction with foreign rule, as well as their spiritual belief in a struggle between the forces of good and evil, fueled

Zhu Yuanzhang, the man who would become the first Ming emperor, had been born into a life of poverty. As a beggar monk, he witnessed the hardships that the common people suffered under Mongol rule.

the Red Turban rebellion. In 1352, a beggar-monk named Zhu Yuanzhang joined one of the Red Turban bands. Zhu Yuanzhang had been born in 1328 in what is today Anhui province. His father had been a landless laborer, but Zhu lost both of his parents to an epidemic in 1344. The orphaned Zhu joined a local Buddhist monastery in an attempt to survive, but was forced to leave when the monastery ran out of food. Zhu survived for three years as a wandering beggar-monk, before returning to the monastery in 1348.

THE THREE TEACHINGS

Religion, as we might know it, did not exist in imperial China. Chinese society did not see a division between the sacred and the secular. Scholars prefer to use the terms "cultural practices," "thought systems," or "philosophies" when discussing the religion of China. Historically, Chinese culture was shaped by the relationships between three philosophies, known as the Three Teachings: Confucianism, Taoism, and Buddhism.

Based on the teachings of Confucius, Confucianism provided ethical guidelines for Chinese political and social interactions since the fifth century BCE. The basic principles of Confucianism stress moral behavior, respect for elders, courtesy, and self-improvement. According to the philosophy behind Taoism, humankind should follow the cosmic flow of the universe, known as Tao, or "the way." Taoism teaches that it is foolish to impose order on the natural world, and that inner peace and balance come only from submitting to the flow of nature.

Unlike Confucianism and Taoism, which were indigenous to China, Buddhism was imported from India. Founded by the Indian prince Siddhartha Gautama, Buddhism was introduced to China in the first century CE by merchants from India. Buddhism spread among China's scholars and aristocrats before becoming popular among the common people. Buddhism teaches that the material world breeds suffering and illusion and that the faithful will be rewarded with enlightenment and salvation.

Although he was barely literate, Zhu Yuanzhang possessed a strategic mind, as well as the ability to make powerful alliances. Zhu recruited brave and talented fighters to his side, earning their loyalty as he led them to victory against other rebel groups and the Yuan army. In 1356, Zhu's army captured Nanjing and, by 1364, had taken control of the entire Yangtze River valley. Whenever Zhu captured a town, he would establish a new civil administration staffed by scholar-officials. He oversaw the revival of agriculture in central China. Zhu also began to distance himself from the Red Turbans, who had established a short-lived dynasty in the north. In 1368, after defeating his rivals, Zhu founded the Ming dynasty and declared himself emperor, assuming the imperial name Hongwu. The Hongwu emperor's first task was to bring the rest of China under his rule. He sent a military expedition north to force out the last of the Mongol court, capturing the Yuan capital Dadu, which was renamed Beiping. The Hongwu emperor also brought Korea and Tibet under Ming rule.

CHAPTER 2

THE RESTORATION OF CHINESE RULE

The Ming dynasty was founded with one basic goal in mind: to return China to the grandeur of the past, to recapture the greatness of the Tang and Song dynasties. Even the dynasty's name, Ming, which means "brilliance," is a reflection of the Hongwu emperor's desire to create what Chinese historian and professor Harold Tanner calls a "stable, harmonious, hierarchical, simple agrarian society, having a strong Han cultural identity, ruled by incorruptible officials and a wise emperor."

The emperor immediately began an enormous effort to restore and revitalize China's economy. As in times past,

The two men in this painting are dressed in the silk robes and hats worn by the upper classes during the Ming dynasty. Ming fashion was based on the styles common in earlier Chinese dynasties.

the revitalization of China's economy under the Ming involved reviving agriculture. Land that had been ruined or abandoned during the rebellion period was resettled, while reservoirs, canals, and dikes were repaired and restored.

The Hongwu emperor also attempted to reshape Ming political and social life. Using a series of autocratic institutions, the emperor sought to replace the system of government that had favored foreigners under the Yuan dynasty with one that would consolidate power among the ethnic Chinese. The emperor also outlawed Mongol names and ordered his people to wear clothing based on Tang fashion. Despite a desire to recapture the glory of older dynasties, however, the Hongwu emperor retained much of the structure of the Yuan bureaucracy.

THE MANDATE OF HEAVEN AND THE ROLE OF THE EMPEROR

The first Ming emperor claimed the right to rule under the Mandate of Heaven. The Mandate of Heaven was an ancient Chinese belief that granted emperors the right to rule. It was first used as justification by the Zhou dynasty to overthrow the Shang dynasty. According to this belief, heaven bestows the right to rule on an emperor who is known as the Son of Heaven. An emperor's claim to the Mandate of Heaven depended on his ability to rule in a manner that demonstrated his goodness and fairness. If an emperor had any personal or political failings, he lost the Mandate of Heaven. Emperors who were removed from power were believed to have lost the Mandate of Heaven.

Under the early Ming system of government, there was very little to differentiate the role of emperor from the role of the emperor under the Yuan dynasty. In the beginning, the Ming dynasty retained the three-branch structure that had been used by the Yuan government. The civil branch of government included a prime minister who oversaw the daily administrative business of the empire, including the six ministries. The military branch of the government retained much of the structure that it had under the Yuan, including an occupational soldier caste and a hereditary office caste. The Censorate was responsible for monitoring administrators at every level for signs of corruption or misconduct.

The earliest years of the Hongwu emperor's reign can be considered a period of caution and moderation. That all ended in 1380, when the emperor accused the prime minister, Hu Weiyong, of conspiracy and treason. Hu Weiyong was executed, along with 30,000 of his supporters in the civil bureaucracy. The role of prime minister was abolished, and the emperor declared that it was to never be restored. The Ming emperor was now the country's chief minister, in direct control of all three branches of the government. The emperor also filled an important religious role in Ming society. The emperor was responsible for overseeing planting and harvest rituals, worshipping Heaven and Earth, and displaying respect and piety towards his ancestors.

SCHOLAR-OFFICIALS AND EUNUCHS

Under the Ming dynasty, the emperor was the autocratic ruler. Under the emperor, the Ming bureaucracy consisted of the highly educated scholar-officials and the palace eunuchs. The scholar-officials came from one of the four classes of Chinese society: the scholars, the farmers and peasants, the artisans and craftsmen, and the merchants. Seen as carrying on the traditions of Confucius, the scholar-officials were responsible for directing the moral education of the people. Before being appointed to government office, a scholar-official would first have to pass a difficult civil service examination. Young men interested in becoming scholar-officials were required to be knowledgeable in classical Chinese literature, poetry, art, ethics, morality, current affairs, and Confucian teachings. They were also one of the few groups in Chinese society who were able to master the difficult writing style of classical Chinese.

After the scholar-officials, those with the most access to

The long robes and hats worn by the scholar-officials of the Ming dynasty indicated their role in the government. This figurine even depicts the mandarin square, a badge worn on the scholar-officials' robes noting their rank.

the Ming emperors were the palace eunuchs. Eunuchs, men who have been castrated, had been a part of Chinese culture for thousands of years, although they were often viewed with contempt and suspicion. The fall of past dynasties were often blamed on eunuchs. With a few exceptions, the role of eunuchs was to serve as the emperor's household servants. Eunuchs, along with the scholar-officials, were the only commoners allowed within the emperor's residence. As personal servants to the emperor and his family, eunuchs could often find themselves in a position to influence policy and gain political favor with the emperor. It has been estimated that roughly 100,000 eunuchs were employed across China under Ming rule.

SOCIAL CLASSES IN MING CHINA

Like many other parts of the world, imperial Chinese society had a hierarchical structure that divided the population into classes. There were four major social classes in imperial China: the *shi*, the *nong*, the *gong*, and the *shang*. China's social hierarchy was based on how important each class was to the society, with the higher ranks having more responsibilities than the lower ones.

The highest status in Chinese society belonged to the *shi*, or the scholars and officials. The *shi* were well-educated and wore silk robes as a sign of their high status. The *shi* worked as advisors, clerks, scribes, and overseers. They filled many administrative roles, performed civil functions, and oversaw the civil service examinations for government positions. The *shi* even commanded troops in battle.

The *nong,* or the farmers and peasants, were the next class in the hierarchy. Because agriculture was vital to Chinese civilization, the *nong* held the second highest rank. Farmers were considered valuable members of society because they fed the entire population. Peasants were important because they were said to work directly for the emperor.

The *gong* were the artisans and craftsmen. The *gong* worked in both the government and private sectors, producing textiles and pottery, and working on architectural projects and public works. Their value to society came from their special skills. The lowest class in Chinese society was the *shang,* or the merchants. The *shang* worked as shopkeepers, traders, bankers, and businessmen. They were considered the lowest class because they did not produce anything for society and earned money from the work of others.

The Ming's first goal was to revive the farmland in central China that had been abandoned or destroyed during the Mongol rule. The Ming believed that agriculture was the foundation of a strong nation.

PROVINCES AND PREFECTURES: ADMINISTRATIVE DIVISIONS IN IMPERIAL CHINA

In the same way that the United States is a country that is divided into states, counties, towns, and cities, imperial China was also divided into smaller sections. Under the Ming, China had four administrative sub-divisions: provinces, prefectures, sub-prefectures, and counties. The empire was divided into thirteen provinces. These provinces were further divided into 159 prefectures, 240 sub-prefectures, and 1,144 counties.

Basic governing was carried out by the magistrates of the 1,144 counties. The magistrates acted as the emperor's surrogates in matters of local government. The responsibilities of the county magistrates included collecting taxes, investigating crimes, apprehending and trying criminals, maintaining public safety, settling civil disputes, and fostering social harmony. County magistrates were aided by the local elites who provided the much-needed manpower to help manage the people, land, and resources of a county. The local elites also assisted in a wide range of social activities, like running schools and organizing local construction projects.

Whatever the level—province, prefecture, sub-prefecture, or county—the division of administration had one goal: to prevent the concentration of power. Keeping power out of the hands of local bureaucrats meant that they could not one day rise up and become a threat to the emperor.

The Ming had a standing army of professional soldiers to defend China from invasions. This statue of a Ming general is a key feature of the Ming Tombs in Beijing.

THE STRENGTH AND STABILITY OF MING RULE

The Ming dynasty ruled China for almost 300 years. In that time, the Ming created a strong central government with the emperor at the center. Using the Mandate of Heaven, the Ming emperors ushered in a period of Ming absolutism, where the emperor was in direct control of the government, the economy, and the military.

The Ming emperors revitalized agriculture and rebuilt the country's infrastructure and defenses. The first emperor crafted a body of law known as the Great Ming Code, which defined a number of laws and listed a range of punishments. This code created a standard legal system to be used by officials and magistrates across the empire. The return of the civil service examinations reversed the unfair political appointment system that had been in effect under the Yuan. Overall, the Ming dynasty was a time of rapid expansion, economic growth, and innovation.

CHAPTER 3

THE GROWTH OF CHINA'S ECONOMY

Under the Mongols, Chinese society had developed into a feudal state, similar to those found in Europe at the time. The emperor rewarded members of the Mongol aristocracy with land and privileges, while the native-born Chinese often lived in poverty and pestilence. This uneven distribution of land was one of the factors leading to the Red Turban rebellions.

The Hongwu emperor, who had risen from the ranks of the poor peasant farmers of the Yuan dynasty, immediately dismantled the feudal system. He resettled peasants and farmers, moving them into lands that had been abandoned during the Mongol rule. Government positions were given to those who were deemed capable, rather than to relatives and vassals. Under the guidance of the autocratic emperor, the four classes of Chinese society flourished, helping Ming China enter into an era of growth and prosperity.

AN EMPIRE OF FARMERS

China is a large country, with a variety of environments and climates, which has helped support various types of agriculture. The plains in the north are cold and dry, with four- to six-month growing seasons suitable for the production of one or two crops per year. The hills and valleys of southern China are warmer and wetter, allowing for a growing season that may last an entire year in which as many as three crops can be produced. Farmers in the north grow wheat and millet (a type of cereal grain), while southern farmers grow rice, tea, and bamboo.

This illustration shows the methods used by Chinese rice farmers during the Ming period. The rice is grown in flooded sections of land called paddy fields.

Farming has always been an important part of Chinese society. During Ming rule, the majority of China's population lived in the countryside and relied on farming to make a living. Furthermore, the farms helped feed the cities, as well as providing goods for merchants and traders to sell.

As the son of a poor farmer, Zhu Yuanzhang had an obvious bias towards the peasant farmers. Many of the Hongwu emperor's initial policies dealt with the redistribution of land to the small farmers. He wanted agriculture to be the source of his new empire's wealth. The emperor promoted development of wastelands by declaring that any farmers who turned them into cultivated land could own the land without it being taxed. The Hongwu emperor also focused on water conservation and irrigation, building or restoring ponds, dikes, and canals all across the empire. In times of peace, soldiers were given land in military settlements that they were expected to use as farmland.

GROWTH OF THE MARKET ECONOMY AND RAPID URBANIZATION

The Hongwu emperor was prejudiced against the merchant class, which was seen as being an unproductive class interested only in attaining wealth. He tried to weaken the merchant class by forcing merchants to pay high taxes and, in some cases, he even tried to relocate them. Despite the Hongwu emperor's prejudice, the merchant class would actually prosper during the reigns of successive emperors. Industry and trade would expand as demand for Chinese manufactured goods, such as porcelain and silk, grew around the world.

The rise in agriculture during the early Ming period led to a surplus of crops. This surplus led to an increase in the market economy, as excess crops could be traded for manufactured goods. The restoration of canals and other waterways during the reign of the first emperor improved transportation, allowing goods to be moved from one end of the empire to the other.

Xian is one of China's oldest cities and the capital of Shaanxi province. Xian was at the eastern end of the Silk Road, making it one of the most important commercial cities in Chinese history.

The manufactured goods that helped give rise to the Ming's market economy began as small cottage industries. A cottage industry is one in which goods are hand-made in the home, often in poor or rural areas. As the need for goods like porcelain and textiles increased, cities and towns grew around the centers of production. The rapid urbanization of these industrial centers was fueled by the crops, which not only fed the rising population, but also provided raw materials for production. Cities along the trade routes—including Beijing, Nanjing, Yangzhou, Suzhou, Guangzhou, Xian, and Chengdu—became prosperous commercial metropolises.

TO INDIA AND AFRICA: THE GROWTH OF FOREIGN TRADE

Prior to the Ming dynasty, China had had an extensive foreign policy and a trade network that stretched from the East China Sea to as far west as Europe. When the Mongols were overthrown, the Hongwu emperor was more interested in consolidating power and revitalizing agriculture in the region than he was in expanding beyond China's existing borders. Later emperors, particularly the Yongle emperor, would pursue an aggressive foreign policy, including extensive exploration and international trade.

Trade fulfilled an important role in the ancient world. In the days before radio, telephones, and the Internet, trade between countries was a means of transmitting thoughts and ideas, as well as exotic goods. Since the time of the Han dynasty, the Silk Road served as the main trade route between the East and West. In the days before reliable maritime navigation and seaworthy vessels, the overland Silk Road was the only means of connecting distant lands. Silk, tea, spices, gems, and medicines were traded along the east-west route. Merchants and pilgrims also traded scientific, philosophical, and cultural knowledge.

THE SEVEN VOYAGES OF ZHENG HE

Zheng He, born Ma Sanbao (later Ma He), was a Muslim who lived in the Yunnan province of southwestern China during the Mongol-led Yuan dynasty. When the Ming dynasty conquered Yunnan, Ma Sanbao was captured, castrated, and sent into the army. He distinguished himself as an officer and diplomat, making influential friends at court.

In 1402, the Yongle emperor wanted to display the Ming's naval superiority and extend trade into the "Western Oceans." Having

This painting of Zheng He appears in a mural near his grave in Yunnan province.

continued on next page

continued from previous page page

become a court eunuch of great influence, Ma He, now renamed Zheng He, was chosen by the emperor to command a fleet of 62 ships on a series of missions to the west. During Zheng He's first voyage in 1405, his fleet visited what is now southern Vietnam, Thailand, Melaka, and Java. The fleet then sailed across the Indian Ocean to Kozhikode, in southern India, and Sri Lanka.

Between 1408 and 1431, Zheng He made an additional six voyages. His fleet sailed past India to the Persian Gulf, the Red Sea, and the east coast of Africa. Zheng He brought envoys from over thirty states in south and southeast Asia to pay tribute to the Chinese emperor. In 1433, during his seventh voyage, Zheng He died. By the time of his death, Zheng He had extended Chinese trade and diplomacy throughout southeast Asia, India, Arabia, and Africa.

By the time the Yongle emperor assumed control of the Ming in 1403, Chinese shipbuilding and navigation had advanced to the point that allowed naval expeditions to sail across the Indian Ocean as far west as Arabia and the eastern coast of Africa. The Chinese combined new technologies and advancements in shipbuilding to expand their influence across the ocean. Magnetic compasses and star charts aided in navigation, adjustable rudders and advanced sail designs improved propulsion, and double-hull designs kept ships from sinking.

CHAPTER 4

RAPID CULTURAL AND SCIENTIFIC DEVELOPMENT

T he reign of the Ming represented a period of rapid cultural developments and scientific advancements. Several factors contributed to this cultural expansion. Similar to the Renaissance in Europe, when artists and thinkers looked to the past of Greece and Rome for inspiration, artists and thinkers of the Ming dynasty drew inspiration from earlier dynastic periods, most notably the southern Song dynasty.

Art and literature flourished under the Ming, especially under the Yongle and Xuande emperors, who were both patrons of the arts. Three of the four great works of classical Chinese literature were written during Ming rule, as were another two well-known novels. Painting, music, poetry, and philosophy also reached new heights in this era. Perhaps the greatest artist achievement of the Ming period is the production of porcelain. Ming-era porcelain is still prized throughout the world today.

Porcelain was first produced in China during the Han dynasty (206 BCE–220 CE). Advances made under Ming rule allowed for the production of new shapes, an array of different colors, and painted designs.

Science and technology also advanced during the almost 300-year Ming reign. The early and middle periods of the dynasty saw numerous accomplishments in the field of medical science. The greatest indication of the era's achievements were the monumental construction projects and large civil engineering works undertaken by the Ming, including the Grand Canal, the Great Wall of China, and the Forbidden City.

LITERATURE, PHILOSOPHY, AND THE ARTS

While traditional forms of literature, such as essays and philosophical treatises, were still produced during the Ming period, the era also saw the development of a new form of literature: the vernacular novel. Traditional literature was written in classical Chinese, which was difficult to learn. Vernacular novels were written in the regional languages of the common people—the vernacular. While only scholar-officials learned classical Chinese, many members of China's new middle class could read and write their regional dialects. Drama and poetry were also popular in the Ming empire. While Ming era poetry tended to imitate the work of poets from past eras, a new form of poetry, similar to the vernacular novel, also developed. Shih-chü songs were a new genre of popular rhyming poetry, written in the vernacular and usually about topics deemed vulgar or inappropriate.

Religion and philosophy were always important aspects of Chinese culture, a trend that continued during the Ming dynasty's rule. The founder of the Ming had been a Buddhist monk before declaring himself emperor, and he remained a follower of Buddhism as emperor. Most of the emperors who followed the Hongwu Emperor were also devoutly Buddhist, although some emperors chose to follow the Taoist faith. Neo-Confucianism, based on philosopher Chu Hsi's critical analysis of classic Confucian texts, had become the dominant philosophy of Ming China. Almost all educated Chinese were fluent in Neo-Confucian thought, which became the basis for the civil service examinations given to aspiring government officials.

Ming China became famous for its handicrafts, including jade and bamboo carvings, silk, paintings, and porcelain. Many of these crafts began as small cottage industries in the countryside. As the economy grew and demand for these handicrafts increased, production moved to factories in or around the rapidly expanding urban centers. Foreign trade also increased demand for Chinese handicrafts and works of art. Ming painting built upon the achievements of earlier Song and Yuan dynasty painting, especially in the area of landscape painting. Ming artists developed new skills and techniques, some of which were influenced by the Chinese art of calligraphy, and several new schools were born across China. Ming painting would also heavily influence painters of the Qing dynasty, as well as those in Japan.

The two commodities that China is perhaps most known for are silk and porcelain. Made from the cocoons of silkworms, silk had been produced in China since at least 4,000 BCE, and the secret of silk production did not leave China until about 140 BCE. Chinese silk was cultivated and spun into fabric that was used for a number of products, including clothing and tapestries. Silk was even used to make an expensive kind of paper. There are examples of books, maps, and paintings all produced on silk. Porcelain had been produced in China since the time of the Tang dynasty, and was always one of the country's biggest commodities; however, the blue and white porcelain of the Ming dynasty has become known around the world. Factories, such as the famed factory at Jingdezhen in the Jiangsu province, could produce enough porcelain plates, bowls, vases, and bottles for the emperor's palace, the growing middle class, and for foreign trade.

The Ming used silk for more than just making clothes. This painting, dating from the 14th century, was created on silk.

SCIENCE, TECHNOLOGY, AND MEDICINE

Although scientific and technological advances and innovations were not on the same level as those of the earlier Tang and Song dynasties, the Ming dynasty was far from stagnant in both regards. A great deal of new scientific and technical concepts were introduced to China through expanded contact with the West, particularly the countries

of Europe, and, while the Chinese did not adopt everything, they did embrace some of the new knowledge. In fact, the vast majority of scientific and technical advances that occurred during the Ming dynasty did not involve the development of new ideas, but rather the modification of existing ones, including agricultural methods and manufacturing technology.

Ruling for twenty-two years, the third Ming emperor, the Yongle Emperor, is often considered the greatest of the Ming rulers. The *Yongle Encyclopedia* was compiled during his reign.

Much of what we know about scientific thought during the Ming dynasty comes from several sources. Compiled during the reign of the Yongle emperor (who ruled from 1402 until 1424), the *Yongle Encyclopedia*, also known as *The Great Canon of the Yongle Era* or the *Vast Documents of the Yongle Era*, contained information on topics such as agriculture, art, astronomy, drama, history, medicine, religion, and technology. The *Yongle Encyclopedia* was the largest known collection of general knowledge in the ancient world and the inspiration for today's modern encyclopedia.

Written by geographer Xu Xiake, *The Travel Diaries Xu Xiake* is considered one of the great works of classical Chinese science and the foundation for the development and study of Chinese geography. Xu Guangpi's *Complete Treatise on Agricultural Management* collects a wealth of agricultural data in a single volume. This compendium discusses subjects such as government agricultural policies and systems, soil and water conservation, animal husbandry, fertilizers, food processing and preparation, and textile and handicraft production. Xu Guangpi's work included numerous technical illustrations of the machinery that was being used in manufacturing and agriculture, making it one of the most important classical works of Chinese agricultural science.

The Ming dynasty also saw various advances in medical science, many of which are still in use today. The Chinese invented variolation, or the inoculation against smallpox using the smallpox virus itself. This practice existed in China for several hundred years before it spread to Europe and the rest of the western world. Li Shizhen, often called the Leonardo da Vinci of China, contributed a great deal to traditional Chinese medicine. He traveled around China and interviewed medical practitioners from across the empire in an attempt to compile all of the available medical knowledge into the most comprehensive text in the world. Li Shizhen's work includes information on and illustrations of over 1,000 medicinal substances. His work has been translated into several languages, including English, Latin, French, and Russian, and is still in use today.

MONUMENTS, TEMPLES, AND TOMBS

From the Great Pyramids of Egypt to the Roman Colosseum, the prosperity and grandeur of a civilization is often reflected in giant construction and engineering projects. Monumental architecture is often a sign of a society's power, wealth, and technical prowess. The Ming dynasty is no different. The Ming dynasty is remembered today for its Great Wall, Grand Canal, and the Forbidden City in Beijing.

Many of the large-scale architectural accomplishments associated with the Ming share a common origin: the Yongle emperor's decision to move China's capital. When the Hongwu emperor founded the Ming dynasty, he established his capital in the southern city of Nanjing, where it would remain for almost forty years. As a young prince, the Yongle emperor had defended China's northern border from the continued threat of the Mongols. When he assumed the throne in 1402, defense of the northern frontier was his top priority. The emperor decided to move China's capital from Nanjing to the northern city of Dadu, the former capital of the Yuan dynasty. Dadu was renamed Beijing, and the emperor began construction of a new palace, the Forbidden City.

This scroll, painted in the mid-15th century, shows the grandeur and mystery of the Forbidden City. The figures at the bottom are commoners, who were not allowed within the city.

THE FORBIDDEN CITY

The Forbidden City, so named because only the emperor, his family, servants, and government officials could enter, is a 178-acre palace complex in Beijing that was home to China's emperors from 1420 to 1911. Construction of the Forbidden City began three years after the Yongle emperor moved China's capital from Nanjing to Beijing. Completed in 1420, the palace complex consists of about 980 wooden buildings roofed with yellow tiles. The complex is surrounded by a wall 32 feet (10 meters) high and a moat 171 feet (52 meters) wide. Three-storied towers stand at each corner of the wall.

Built along a north-south axis, the Forbidden City is divided into an outer court and an inner court. The outer court consists of the Hall of Supreme Harmony, the Hall of Central Harmony, and the Hall of Preserving Harmony. Most official government business was carried out in the outer court. The inner court, which served as the residences for the emperor and his household, consisted of the Hall of Heavenly Purity, the Hall of Union, and the Hall of Earthly Tranquility.

The Forbidden City served as the home of twenty-four emperors from both the Ming and the Qing dynasties. An uprising in 1911 forced the last Qing emperor, the 5-year-old Puyi, to flee the Forbidden City. Puyi officially abdicated the following year, ending China's imperial period. In 1925, the Palace Museum was established in the Forbidden City. Today, the Palace Museum is the largest museum of Chinese cultural and historical relics from the Shang dynasty through to the Qing dynasty.

In addition to the Forbidden City, the Ming rulers would build several other magnificent buildings, shrines, and temples. Built between 1406 and 1420, the Temple of Heaven is a complex of religious buildings in southeastern Beijing. The Temple of Heaven is where the emperors performed the annual ceremonies of prayer to heaven, which were intended to ensure a good harvest. In the 16th century, the Jiajing emperor extended the complex, adding three other temples: The Temple of Sun, the Temple of Earth, and the Temple of Moon. Another important religious site in the area are the Imperial Tombs of the Ming and Qing dynasties. As the first emperor to live in Beijing, the Yongle emperor chose a site just north of the city, on the southern slope of Tianshou Mountain, for his tomb. Over time, other Ming emperors built their tombs in the same area, eventually creating a necropolis, or "city of the dead." The elaborate burial site included the Spirit Way, a 4-mile (7-kilometer) road, lined with statues of guardian animals and important officials, and a

Like Egyptian pharaohs, the Ming emperors were buried in elaborate tombs. This red gate leads to the statue-lined Spirit Way, a central feature of the Ming Tombs.

three-arched gate known as the Great Red Gate. The site also includes a number of pillars, statues, gates, and arches, including one of the largest stone archways in China.

The Yongle emperor's decision to move the capital to Beijing directly led to the largest civil engineering projects of the Ming period: the Grand Canal and the Great Wall. At 1,104 miles (1776 kilometers) long, the Grand Canal, is the longest canal in the world. Although it had existed in

Jiayuguan Pass is the western-most point of the Ming Great Wall. The fortress at Jiayuguan Pass is the most intact fortification along the wall today.

one form or another since the fifth century BCE, it was the Ming who repaired, revitalized, and expanded the canal. The Grand Canal begins in Beijing and travels south, ending at Hangzhou, connecting the Yellow River and the Yangtze River. It served as one of the most important internal trade routes of Ming China.

Like the Grand Canal, the Great Wall had existed in other forms throughout Chinese history, although it was under the Ming that it would take the shape that is most familiar today. The earlier walls were mostly made of earth and stone. Faced with the ongoing threat of Mongol invasion from the north, the Ming extended the wall, which would eventually come to stretch across more than 12,000 miles (20,000 kilometers) and span nine provinces. The reconstruction included redesigning many of the towers and fortifications that stood along the length of the wall, as well as adding cannons to some strategic locations. In certain sections, most notably west of Beijing, the Great Wall splits into two lines, the Inner Wall to the south and the Outer Wall to the north, providing an additional layer of defense. The Ming kept the wall heavily garrisoned with soldiers, who manned the battlements, gates, and signal towers that ran along its length. Today, although many sections have fallen into disrepair, the Great Wall of China remains a symbol of China, as well as a testament to the strength and skill of the Ming dynasty.

CHAPTER 5

THE DECLINE AND FALL
OF THE MING

No empire, regardless of its size or achievements, can last forever. Like the Egyptians, Romans, and Persians before them, the empire of the Ming dynasty would one day fall into decline. Although the early Ming rulers ushered in a new era of growth and prosperity, the emperors of the later periods were unable to manage many of the fundamental changes brought on by that growth.

The strong, autocratic central government that had been established by the Hongwu emperor served to stabilize China following the defeat of the Yuan dynasty. However, the weak and ineffectual emperors of the later periods could not handle the reins of power. Their weaknesses led to political infighting between the scholar-officials, government ministers, and palace eunuchs. Furthermore, shifts in China's economy, reliance on foreign trade, and various natural disasters all led to the eventual collapse of the Ming dynasty.

WEAK EMPERORS, PLOTTING EUNUCHS, AND FOREIGN TRADE

The Hongwu emperor had spent his reign consolidating political power. He abolished the position of prime minister and took direct control of the civil government. The emperor had a vision of a stable nation, built upon the traditions of classical Chinese culture. The Ming established a strong central government backed by a universal code of law.

The emperors of the early Ming period were able to continue the strength and stability of the Hongwu emperor's reign. Later emperors, some still children when they came to power, were incapable of carrying on the tradition of autocratic rule. These later rulers were often more interested in the comforts of palace life than in the day-to-day job of running a country. The incompetent and disinterested emperors relied more and more on the scholar-officials to handle the affairs of state. The palace eunuchs also found themselves in a new position of political influence. The Hongwu emperor distrusted eunuchs and made sure that they had little influence at court. His successors, on the other hand, revived the eunuchs' role in the government. Factions would develop among the scholar-officials and the palace eunuchs, as both sides tried to use their access to the emperor to influence political decisions. These divisions became especially telling during the reign of the Wanli emperor, who held power from 1572 until 1620. The Chongzhen emperor, the last Ming ruler, tried to reverse the damage caused by these divisions, but his efforts were in vain.

The Ming dynasty's stable government had led to an economic boom. The early emperors' focus on revitalizing China's agricultural production fueled population growth, industry, and the development of the merchant class. According to the classical Chinese model, merchants belonged to the lowest class in Chinese society. However, after decades of increased foreign trade and the growth of a free market, the merchant class had become wealthy and powerful. The power and prosperity of the merchant class led to a blurring of the lines between the social classes. The merchant and farmer classes became cultured and literate, allowing members of these classes to pass the civil service examinations and gain access to government positions and the influence that came with them.

The Ming dynasty had been founded as an agrarian society, an

The Chongzhen Emperor, seen here with Empress Zhuang Lie Min, was unable to save the once-strong Ming government from political factions and infighting. He would be the last emperor of the Ming dynasty.

empire built on agriculture. By the end of the dynasty, the Chinese economy had become too reliant on trade with foreign nations. The seventeenth century saw a number of economic setbacks that had a negative impact on the Ming's global trade network. The decrease in global trade had a huge effect on China's economy, which had come to rely on Europe's goods and silver.

DISEASE, FAMINE, AND THE LITTLE ICE AGE

China, like the rest of eastern Eurasia, is a patchwork of tectonic plates, making it prone to earthquakes. Ming China was struck by a number of earthquakes in the 1440s, 1480s, and between 1505 and 1528. A devastating earthquake hit on January 23, 1556, in Zhaocheng. Said to have measured an 8 on the Richter scale, this earthquake leveled city walls, buildings, and homes in the Yellow River Valley. According to Ming scholar Timothy Brook, the Shaanxi and Shanxi provinces "continued to shake for a month," and an estimated 830,000 people lost their lives. Another powerful earthquake struck in December 1604. This time, the earthquake hit along China's southeast coast, destroying two important seaports in that region.

During the first half of the 1600s, China was affected by climate changes brought about by the Little Ice Age, a period of global cooling that occurred between 1300 and 1870. The Little Ice Age brought cold, dry weather to northern China, which greatly shortened the growing season. The late Ming period also saw China hit by a number of devastating droughts and floods. The various environmental disasters led to crop failure and famine.

In addition to these environmental disasters, China in the late Ming period was also struck by an epidemic. Epidemics were not uncommon, as poor sanitation and unhealthy practices made it easy to spread disease through crowded populations. There were several outbreaks during the Ming period in the early 1400s and again in the late 1500s. A final epidemic occurred during the last six years of Ming rule. Historians are unsure which disease was responsible for these outbreaks, although many believe it was a combination of dysentery, typhoid fever, smallpox, and plague. The combination of natural disasters, crop failures, and epidemics led many Chinese to assume that the Ming dynasty had finally lost the Mandate of Heaven.

REBELLION, INVASION, AND THE LEGACY OF THE MING

Much like the rebellions that occurred towards the end of the Yuan dynasty and led to the rise of the Ming, the late period of the Ming dynasty saw popular rebellions and uprisings spread across the country. Many regions, especially in the north of China, had been hit with famine and poverty due to the environmental and economic collapse of the early seventeenth century. Things were so bad that, as Chinese historian and professor Harold Tanner states, many starving people "sold their children and were reduced to eating bark and earth," some even resorting to cannibalism to survive. There was an increase in banditry, with many bandit gangs often joining together to form rebel armies. Two of the main rebel forces were led by a village leader named Li Zicheng and peasant warlord Zhang Xianzhog. Li Zicheng attracted the powerful middle class to his side, establishing his own dynasty in Xiangyang. He marched on Beijing, conquering the city. After the city was captured, the Chongzhen emperor—that last Ming ruler—killed himself. Zhang Xianzhog led bands of raiders in the northwest. His forces conquered Sichuan in west-central China, and he declared himself King of the Great Western Kingdom. Many of these rebel bands succeeded because the men responsible for stopping them—the soldiers and officers of the military—were abandoning their posts. The collapse of the Ming economy left many soldiers unpaid. Forced to contend with poverty and starvation, unpaid soldiers left their posts and joined rebel bands.

The collapse of the military left Ming China open to invasion from outside forces, just as it was also trying to subdue popular rebellions at home. For over one hundred years, Japanese pirates had raided the coast of China. Although the Ming were eventually able to put an end to Japanese pirate raids, the threat from Japan continued, culminating in a series of invasions of the Chinese mainland known as the Imjin War.

The rough seas and unexpected current changes helped the Korean navy defeat the much larger Japanese fleet at the Battle of Myeongnyang, part of the Imjin War between China and Japan.

THE IMJIN WAR

The Imjin War, which lasted from 1592 until 1598, set the foundation for international relations between China, Korea, and Japan for the next 400 years. Toyotomi Hideyoshi, the warlord who had united Japan after centuries of civil war, wanted to conquer mainland China. Land in Japan was scarce and Hideyoshi needed land to offer his restless supporters in order to maintain control. The easiest way for Hideyoshi's forces to reach China was through the Korean peninsula.

The Korean forces were no match for Hideyoshi's samurai-led army. Korea's ally, Ming China, sent a force of 5,000 troops, that was easily defeated by the Japanese invaders. Despite initial success, Japan's victory was delayed when the Korean admiral Yi Sunshin cut off the Japanese navy from supplying its troops on the mainland. In 1593, China sent another 30,000 soldiers to reclaim the northern section of the Korean peninsula. China and Japan entered into a series of diplomatic talks that lasted years. Japan launched a second wave of invasion in October 1597. After another year of fighting, the Japanese army began to withdraw, with the last of the Japanese forces departing Korea on December 24, 1598.

While the Ming focused on threats from outside forces, notably the Japanese and the constant threat of Mongol invasion from the north, the real threat to the continuation of the dynasty came from within the empire's borders. Manchuria in the northeast had been under Ming rule since 1387. The Manchus were hunters and farmers who occasionally engaged in trade with the Ming. Starting in the 1580s, a chieftain named Nurhaci began unifying the different Jurchen tribes of the region, creating the Manchu state. The Manchus began making alliances with Ming officials in the north, eventually leading a successful raid across the Great Wall into northern China. The Manchus subdued the Mongols, defeated the Yi dynasty in Korea, and captured several cities in northern China before taking control of Beijing, which had been under the control of Li Zicheng's rebel army.

In 1636, Nurhaci's son Hong Taiji founded the Qing dynasty and named himself emperor. Between the rebellions and the Manchu invasion, the Ming government was forced to flee the north. The Manchu forces moved south, gaining supporters and consolidating their power. Zhu Youlang, the grandson of a Ming emperor, tried

Hong Taiji, son of the Manchu chieftain Nurhaci, founded the Qing dynasty in 1644. China would never again have another ethnic Chinese dynasty.

to revive Ming rule in southern China and was declared emperor. However, he eventually fled to Burma and was finally captured and executed in 1662.

After the Manchu conquest, life in China went on much as it had during the Ming dynasty. The Qing dynasty adopted many of the institutions, policies, and laws of the Ming. The economic, cultural, and intellectual traditions that had existed in the late Ming period continued into the Qing reign.

The Ming dynasty was born of a desire to recapture the traditions of the past and to create a new empire based on the ethnic Han ideal. The Ming emperors created a vast nation, fueled by agriculture and supported by industry and trade. Ming art and handicrafts are still prized around the world, while monuments like the Great Wall and the Forbidden City are recognized landmarks and symbols of Chinese greatness. So much of what we consider to be "traditionally Chinese" comes from the Ming dynasty, and that may be the Ming's greatest legacy.

TIMELINE

c. 1600–1046 BCE The first recorded state, the Shang dynasty, unites most of north-central China.

1045–770 BCE The Zhou dynasty replaces the Shang in northern China.

c. 770 BCE The Zhou dynasty collapses and is replaced by a series of warring states, known as the eastern Zhou dynasty.

221–06 BCE King Ying Zheng unites most of central China as the Qin dynasty. Zheng becomes first ruler in China to use the title "emperor." The First Great Wall of China is built.

206 BCE–220 CE The Han dynasty ushers in China's first "golden age." Confucianism becomes state philosophy. Buddhism first appears in China.

220–589 The Han dynasty collapses. China is ruled by competing dynasties for almost 400 years. Dynasties begin to develop in southern China.

581–618 China is reunited under the Sui dynasty.

618–907 Under the Tang dynasty, imperial China extends into central Asia for the first time.

960–1279 The Song dynasty ushers in an era of classical literature and scientific innovation.

1271–1368 The Mongols invade and conquer China. Kublai Khan establishes the Yuan dynasty. Marco Polo and other westerners visit imperial China.

1350s The Red Turban movement and other peasant rebellions openly protest Mongol rule.

1368 The Mongols are overthrown. Zhu Yuanzhang is named the first emperor of the Ming and takes the imperial title the Hongwu emperor. In Nanjing, the Ming establish a strong central government supported by a sophisticated agricultural economy.

14th–17th centuries The Great Wall of China, as it is known today, is built.

1402 The Yongle emperor becomes the third Ming emperor.

1403 The capital city is moved from Nanjing to Beijing.

TIMELINE

1411–15 The Grand Canal is restored, linking the Yellow River and the Yangtze River.

1500–1850 The Little Ice Age, a period of global climate change that led to droughts, crop failures, and famine around the world, triggers natural disasters around China.

1572 The Wanli emperor assumes control of the Ming. Political factionalism in his court leads to abuses of power by scholar-officials and eunuchs.

1592–98 A series of conflicts known as the Imjin War pit China and Korea against Japan.

1627 The Chongzhen emperor, the last Ming ruler, takes power.

1644 The Ming dynasty is replaced by the Manchu Qing dynasty. Imperial China expands with the annexation of Tibet and Mongolia.

19th century The Qing dynasty begins a long decline. The central government weakens as regional warlords rise in power.

1899–1901 The "Boxer Rebellion" attempts to drive out foreigners and re-establish traditional imperial rule. Defeated by foreign intervention from the West, Russia, and Japan, weakens the Qing government.

1911–12 Military revolts lead to the end of imperial rule and the creation of the Republic of China.

GLOSSARY

abdicate Voluntarily give up one's throne, power, or responsibility.

agrarian Relating to land, its ownership, or farming.

autocratic Pertaining to a form of government in which a single person has unlimited power.

battlement A low wall at the top of a castle or tower with open spaces for people inside to shoot through.

calligraphy Decorative handwriting or lettering produced with a brush or pen.

caste A social class that is based on family, profession, or economic status.

castrate To remove reproductive organs.

censorial Relating to an office or official responsible for examining books, plays, news reports, etc., for the purpose of suppressing what is deemed objectionable.

commodity A material or agricultural product that can be bought and sold.

compendium A collection of various items, such as photos or facts, often presented in the form of a printed book.

cultivate To prepare for the growing of crops.

dialect A particular way of speaking a language, often based upon geography or social class.

epidemic A sudden and rapidly spreading outbreak of disease.

free market An economic system in which the prices are based on competition among businesses and not set by the government.

hierarchy A system of ranking people or things, in which some certain groups are above others.

infrastructure The basic facilities and systems serving a country, city, or area, such as transportation and communication systems.

monastery The residence of a group of people living together in seclusion under religious vows.

necropolis A historic or prehistoric burial site, especially one with monumental architecture.

GLOSSARY

pestilence A deadly and overwhelming disease that often affects an entire community or area.

prefecture A regional political subdivision controlled by local government.

secular Not controlled by or related to a church or other religious institution.

shrine A holy place or structure devoted to prayer or pilgrimage.

stagnant Characterized by a lack of progress, development, or advancement.

tectonic plate A section of the outer layer of the Earth whose movement and interaction with other plates shapes and changes the Earth's surface.

vernacular Related to everyday, rather than formal, speech.

Asian Art Museum
200 Larkin Street
San Francisco, CA 94102
(415) 581-3500
Website: http://www.asianart.org
The Asian Art Museum is home to a vast collection of art and arti-
facts from around Asia, including pieces from the Ming era. The
museum also hosts events and programs for visitors of all ages.

The Canadian Society for Asian Arts
260-5655 Cambie Street
Vancouver, BC V5Z 3A4
Canada
(604) 689-2755
Website: http://canadiansocietyforasianarts.org/
The Canadian Society for Asian Arts is a nonprofit multicultural organization devoted to Asian arts and cultures. The Society promotes
the appreciation and understanding of the arts of Asia through
special programs, exhibitions, and publications.

China Institute in America
100 Washington Street
New York, NY 1006
(212) 744-8181
Website: http://www.chinainstitute.org/
Founded in 1926 by a group of American and Chinese educators,
the China Institute is the oldest bicultural organization in America
devoted to promoting awareness of Chinese culture and heritage.
The China Institute promotes an understanding of China through
programs in education, culture, business, and art.

Chinese Cultural Center of Greater Vancouver
Museum & Archives
555 Columbia Street
Vancouver, BC V64 4H5
Canada

FOR MORE INFORMATION

(604) 658-8880
Website: http://www.cccvan.com/
The Chinese Cultural Center of Greater Vancouver promotes
   Chinese art and culture within the multicultural landscape of mod-
   ern Canada. In addition to cultural and community events, the
   Chinese Cultural Center also runs a museum and a Chinese lan-
   guage school of over 4,000 students.

Chinese Historical Society of America (CHSA)
965 Clay Street
San Francisco, CA 94108
(415) 391-1188
Website: http://chsa.org/
The CHSA is the oldest organization in the United States to promote
   and preserve the social, political, and cultural contributions of the
   Chinese in the United States. The CHSA provides exhibitions, publications, and educational programs, as well as tours, film
   screenings, readings, and workshops.

National Geographic Society
1145 17th Street NW
Washington, DC 20036
(202) 857-7000
Website: http://www.nationalgeographic.com/
The National Geographic Society is one of the largest nonprofit
   science and educational organizations in the world. It promotes
   environmental and historical conservation through advancing the
   study of geography, archaeology, and natural science.

The World Heritage Centre
UNESCO
7, Place de Fontenoy
75352 Paris CEDEX 07
France
+33 (0)1 45 68 24 96
Website: http://whc.unesco.org/

Part of the United Nations Educational, Scientific and Cultural
   Organization (UNESCO), the World Heritage Centre is responsible
   for protecting sites of historical importance around the world.

The World History Organization
Meserve Hall
Northeastern University
360 Huntington Avenue
Boston, MA 02130
(617) 373-6818
Website: http://www.thewha.org/
The World History Organization promotes the study of world his-
   tory from a cross-cultural, comparative, and global approach.
   Secondary educators, college and university professors, graduate
   students, and independent scholars work together to prepare stu-
   dents and the public for an interdependent, multicultural world.

WEBSITES

Because of the changing nature of Internet links, Rosen
Publishing has developed an online list of websites related
to the subject of this book. This site is updated regularly.
Please use this link to access this list:
http://www.rosenlinks.com/RFE/ming

FOR FURTHER READING

Dawson, Patricia A. *Asia Through the Ages: Early History to European Colonialism*. New York, NY: Cavendish Square, 2015.

Hollihan-Elliot, Sheila. *Ancient History of China*. Broomall, PA: Mason Crest, 2013.

Hollihan-Elliot, Sheila. *Art and Architecture of China*. Broomall, PA: Mason Crest, 2013.

Jenson-Elliott, Cindy. *Ancient Chinese Dynasties*. San Diego, CA: ReferencePoint Press, 2015.

Jenson-Elliott, Cindy. *The Great Wall of China*. San Diego, CA: ReferencePoint Press, 2014.

Liao, Yan. *Famous People of China*. Broomall, PA: Mason Crest, 2013.

Lu, Jia. *The Geography of China*. Broomall, PA: Mason Crest, 2013.

Mah, Adeline Yen. *China: Land of Dragons and Emperors*. New York, NY: Random House, 2011.

Perritano, John. *China: Tradition, Culture, and Daily Life*. Broomall, PA: Mason Crest, 2016.

Roberts, J.A.G. *A History of China*. London, England: Palgrave Macmillan, 2011.

Rosinsky, Natalie M. *Ancient China*. Mankato, MN: Compass Point Books, 2013.

Slavicek, Louise Chipley. *The Great Wall of China*. New York, NY: Chelsea House, 2005.

Snedden, Robert. *Ancient China*. Mankato, MN: The Creative Company, 2011.

Sonneborn, Liz. *Ancient China*. New York, NY: Children's Press, 2012.

Temple, Robert. *The Genius of China: 3,000 Years of Science, Discovery, and Invention*. Rochester, VT: Inner Traditions/Bear & Company, 2007.

BIBLIOGRAPHY

Brook, Timothy. *The Troubled Empire: China in the Yuan and Ming Dynasties*. Cambridge, MA: Harvard University Press, 2010.

Burgan, Michael. *Empire of the Mongols*. New York, NY: Facts On File, 2005.

Cai, Helen. "Ethnic Groups in China: A History and Comparison." *Duke East Asia Nexus*. Retrieved November 30, 2015 (http://www.dukenex.us/helen-cai-ethnic-groups-in-china-a-history-and-a-comparison.html).

China Internet Information Center. "The Thirteen Ming Tombs in Beijing." Retrieved December 1, 2015 (http://www.china.org.cn/english/features/atam/115650.htm).

Dardess, John W. *Ming China, 1368-1644: A Concise History of a Resilient Empire*. Lanham, MD: Rowman and Littlefield, 2012.

Department of Asian Art. "Scholar-Officials of China." The Metropolitan Museum of Art. Retrieved November 28, 2015 (http://www.metmuseum.org/toah/hd/schg/hd_schg.htm).

Dersin, Denise, ed. *What Life Was Like in the Land of the Dragon: Imperial China AD 960–1368*. Richmond, VA: Time-Life Books, 1998.

Doran, Christine. "Chinese Palace Eunuchs: Shadows of the Emperor." *Nebula* 7.3 (2010): 11-26.

Fessenden, Marissa. "More than 1,200 Miles of China's Great Wall Have Been Destroyed." *Smithsonian*, July 2015 (http://www.smithsonianmag.com/smart-news/erosion-and-human-damage-have-destroyed-more-1200-miles-chinas-great-wall-180955810/?no-ist).

Gelber, Harry G. *The Dragon and the Foreign Devils: China and the World, 1100 BC to the Present*. New York, NY: Walker Publishing, 2007.

Hadingham, Evan. "Ancient Chinese Explorers." NOVA, January 16, 2001 (http://www.pbs.org/wgbh/nova/ancient/ancient-chinese-explorers.html).

Hansen, Valerie. *The Silk Road: A New History*. New York, NY: Oxford University Press, 2012.

Jenson-Elliott, Cindy. *Ancient Chinese Dynasties*. San Diego, CA: ReferencePoint Press, 2015.

BIBLIOGRAPHY

Larmer, Brook. "The Great Wall of China Is Under Siege."
  Smithsonian, August 2008 (www.smithsonianmag.com
  /people-places/the-great-wall-of-china-is-under-siege-825452
  /?no-list).

Man, John. *The Great Wall: The Extraordinary Story of China's
  Wonder of the World*. Cambridge, MA: Da Capo Press, 2008.

The Mariner's Museum. "Exploration Through the Ages." Retrieved
  November 29, 2015 (ageofex.marinersmuseum.ord/index.php).

Morton, W. Scott and Charlton M. Lewis. *China: Its History and
  Culture*. New York, NY: McGraw-Hill, 2004.

Nuwer, Rachel. "Six Centuries Ago, Chinese Explorers Left This Coin
  Behind in Africa." *Smithsonian*, March 2013 (http://www
  .smithsonianmag.com/smart-news/six-centuries-ago-chinese
  -explorers-left-this-coin-behind-in-africa-2810588/).

Roberts, J.A.G. *A Concise History of China*. Cambridge, MA:
  Harvard University Press, 1999.

Schultz, Colin. "Archaeologists Chart the First Great Wall of China."
  Smithsonian, January 2014 (http://www
  .smithsonianmag.com/smart-news/archaeologists-chart-first-great
  -wall-china-180949347/).

Springer, Brandon. "A Thousand Years of Art Under China's
  Emperors." *Smithsonian,* July 2010 (http://www.smithsonianmag
  .com/smithsonian-institution/a-thousand-years-of-art-under-chinas
  -emperors-139611648/).

UNESCO. "Temple of Heaven: An Imperial Sacrificial Altar in
  Beijing." Retrieved December 1, 2015 (whc.unesco.org/en
  /list/881).

INDEX

INDEX

invasions of, 6–13, 41, 49
names, 15

P

philosophy, of the Ming dynasty, 5, 10, 12, 27, 29, 31–33
population growth, 4, 44
porcelain, 25, 26, 29, 32–33
private industry, 4, 25, 26, 32, 44, 51

Q

Qing dynasty, 5, 32, 38, 39, 50, 51

R

Red Turban rebellions, 11–12, 13, 22

S

scholar-officials, 13, 17–18, 31, 43
science, during Ming dynasty, 30, 34–36
Shang dynasty, 15, 38
silk, 25, 27, 32
Silk Road, 26–27
Six Ministries, 9–10, 16
social classes, in Ming China, 18–19
Song dynasty, 8, 9, 10, 14, 29, 32, 34
steppes, 4, 6

T

Tang dynasty, 14, 32–33, 34
fashion, 15
Taoism, 11, 12, 13, 31

technology, during Ming dynasty, 28, 30, 34–36

U

urbanization, 4, 24–26

X

Xuande emperor, 29

Y

Yi dynasty, 50
Yinchuan, 7
Yongle emperor, 26, 27, 28, 29, 35, 36, 38, 39, 40
Yongle Encyclopedia, 35
Yuan dynasty, 7–9, 15, 16, 21, 22, 27, 42, 46
    army of, 13
    art of, 32
    capital of, 13, 37
    emperors of, 11
    establishment of, 4
    government of, 9, 16
    overthrow of, 4

Z

Zhang Xianzhog, 47
Zheng He, 27–28
Zhou dynasty, 15
Zhu Yuanzhang, 12, 13, 24
    as Hongwu emperor, 13, 14, 15, 16, 22, 24, 26, 31, 36, 42, 43
    and the peasant uprising, 11–13
Zhu Youlang, 50–51

ABOUT THE AUTHOR

Growing up in New York City, Daniel R. Faust took advantage of the city's many art and history museums. Weekends at the American Museum of Natural History, Metropolitan Museum of Art, and Brooklyn Museum helped build a lifelong interest in history and world cultures. After receiving separate degrees in archaeology and English literature, he taught history in the New York City public school system and literature at the City University of New York, before turning his attention to writing children's nonfiction.

PHOTO CREDITS

Designer: Brian Garvey; Editor: Shalini Saxena: Photo Researcher: Nicole Baker